World's Best "True" UFO Stories

Jenny Randles &
Peter A. Hough

Illustrated by Jason Hurst

Sterling Publishing Co., Inc.
New York

Library of Congress Cataloging-in-Publication Data

Randles, Jenny.
     World's best "true" UFO stories / by Jenny Randles and Peter A.
Hough ; illustrated by Jason Hurst.
          p.   cm.
     Includes index.
     ISBN 0-8069-1258-8
     1. Unidentified flying objects—Sightings and encounters—Juvenile
literature.   [1. Unidentified flying objects.]   I. Hough, Peter A.
II. Hurst, Jason, ill.   III. Title.
TL789.R345   1994
001.9'42—dc20   94

10   9   8   7   6   5   4   3

First paperback edition published in 1995 by
Sterling Publishing Company, Inc.
387 Park Avenue South, New York, N.Y. 10016
© 1994 by Jenny Randles & Peter A. Hough
Distributed in Canada by Sterling Publishing
% Canadian Manda Group, One Atlantic Avenue, Suite 105
Toronto, Ontario, Canada M6K 3E7
Distributed in Great Britain and Europe by Cassell PLC
Wellington House, 125 Strand, London WC2R 0BB, England
Distributed in Australia by Capricorn Link (Australia) Pty Ltd.
P.O. Box 6651, Baulkham Hills, Business Centre, NSW 2153, Australia
Manufactured in the United States of America
All rights reserved

Sterling ISBN 0-8069-1258-8 Trade
0-8069-1259-6 Paper

Contents

Before You Begin

The title of this book is *World's Best "True" UFO Stories.* It was a tough job picking out the "world's best." Indeed, there were many we had to leave out due to shortage of space and the need to vary the stories. But we believe the book includes some of the best-documented cases available.

"True" in the title is in quotation marks because often "truth" is a personal judgment. What one person will accept as truth, others may refuse because they demand more proof. In the cases we present here, there are varying degrees of proof. Sometimes the evidence is so overwhelming, as in "Landing at Socorro" or "Danger on the Highway," that you may wonder why some people still deny the existence of UFOs. In other accounts, such as "Fire in the Sky" and "The Alien on Ilkley Moor," you may be more critical.

We are professional UFOlogists and the authors of many other books on UFOs and similar subjects. But we are not "believers" in the sense that we swallow everything without question. We would like you to be the same. Ask questions about people's strange stories. It is fair to demand some proof that an incident happened in the way it was reported.

However, do not forget to ask questions of the "unbelievers," too, the skeptics and debunkers. They can be just as guilty in obscuring facts that do not fit in with their "rational" explanations.

Finally, we would just like to say, read on and enjoy the world's best "true" UFO stories . . .

1. CLOSE ENCOUNTERS OF THE FIRST KIND— STRANGE SIGHTINGS

- UFOs in another age . . .
- The flying saucer gets its name—by mistake . . .
- Not only pilots and farmers see UFOs, presidents can, too . . .
- When you see a UFO—keep your distance!

Encounter in 1909

Starting in the 1880s, a plague of mysterious "airships" swept across North America and Europe and as far away as New Zealand. One of the most interesting cases occurred in 1909.

Mr. C. Lethbridge was travelling around Wales during the summer with his Punch and Judy show, packed on a handtruck. As he walked over Caerphilly Mountain, he saw a sight that frightened him.

"At first I thought it was a big bird," he told reporters later. "I saw a funny-looking object on the roadside, and two men who seemed to be at some kind of work close by. The object was long and like a big cigar. They were tall men, military-looking men, and were dressed in thick fur coats and caps. Of course, I didn't know they were officers, but they were two men—that's certain, and military men, too.

"I was about 20 or 30 yards away when I first saw the men. The noise of my truck—it rattles a lot—must have disturbed them for they commenced to speak very fast, some kind of lingo which I could not understand. They appeared to pick up something off the ground and jump into the object close by. Then it rose up like—like a switchback movement—and when it had got up a pretty good height, it went straight in the direction of Cardiff.

"I thought at first it was some big bird, but it must have been an airship. Well, after it had gone up a way, two lights began to shine from it. They looked like electric lights. It made an awful noise—a whirring noise—a noise like an engine working. Saw and heard it! I have no doubt about it. I was frightened, I can tell you, and after watching it go away towards Cardiff, I continued to walk home."

Lethbridge's strange experience took place between 10:30 and 11 o'clock on Tuesday night, May 18th. Interestingly, it was confirmed by the statements of residents in Salisbury Road, Cathays, Cardiff, who said that they also saw an object in the air that looked like an airship between 10:40 and 10:50 P.M.

Then the *South Wales Daily News* of May 20 referred to several Cardiff dock workmen who sighted an airship in the wee hours of Wednesday morning.

Lethbridge's vague description of the object as "long and like a big cigar" has often been used in modern UFO accounts.

A search was made on Caerphilly Mountain at the location that Lethbridge indicated, and a red label printed in French was discovered, along with a piece of mutilated notepaper and several other slips of paper, but these only served to confuse the issue.

At the time, it was thought that the airships had been built secretly by inventors, or that they were flying machines belonging to foreign powers. Neither was the case, since the objects had capabilities beyond the technology of the time. The sightings and encounters differed only slightly from present-day UFO experiences.

The First "Flying Saucer"

The early afternoon of June 24, 1947, was fine and sunny over the western United States. Pilot Kenneth Arnold flew slowly over the splendid Cascade Mountains, heading towards Pendleton, Oregon. He was enjoying the peace and loneliness of the air as his small plane buffeted in the wind.

Suddenly his attention was drawn by a glint of light, followed swiftly by another, then a third. He looked towards Mount Baker and there saw a formation of nine strange aircraft swishing across the sky.

He was baffled by their odd form. He'd never seen anything like it. At first he thought they might be reflections of the sun on the cockpit window, so he wound that down and drank in the rushing blast of cold air. The strange craft were still there.

They were moving together on a steady course and had a weird appearance. Their wings were curved and shaped like a crescent moon. Arnold told himself they had to be some newfangled aircraft that the government was testing. He watched them with the admiration and respect that one pilot gives to another in a vastly superior machine.

Lining up the group against the top of a mountain peak, he started to time them on his dashboard clock. He worked out the distance between one peak and another, which they covered remarkably quickly.

Arnold did a rough calculation in his head to figure out their speed. Then he checked it again. It didn't make sense. The objects were flying much faster than any aircraft he had ever heard about. Perhaps they were some kind of rocket or missile. If so, then he sure hoped that they were Uncle Sam's!

When he landed for a brief stop at Yakima in Washington state, he mentioned what he'd seen to some people on the ground. By the time he had flown on to Pendleton, he was greeted by newspaper and radio reporters. Everybody wanted to know about the strange machines.

Arnold told them about his sighting. He had

guessed that the things were 20 miles away. If he was right, it meant that their speed was fantastic. Later he was told by experts that if they had been that far away, their size would have been absolutely enormous. At that distance, even the largest aircraft ever built would have been impossible to see without binoculars. Arnold had pretty good eyesight, but not that good!

But, however fast they flew, the objects were still very unusual in design, and they had bounced through the air in a most peculiar way. Arnold told one reporter that they skimmed across the sky "like a saucer would if you skipped it across water"—the same way a small flat stone would if you threw it at a sharp angle.

Arnold's choice of words was to prove fateful. The reporter called the objects "flying saucers." He wrote his story telling the world that aerial intruders had arrived. As a result, many people began to look up into the sky for them.

Of course, most of those who read the newspaper story imagined that Arnold had seen things shaped like saucers, when they had not resembled saucers at all. Yet witnesses now started reporting saucer-shaped objects, and comic books and films featured this image regularly.

The "flying saucer" had gripped the popular imagination. A simple mistake made by a newspaper writer became the origin of a legend.

Mr. President Spots a UFO

Anybody can see a UFO. You simply have to be in the right place at the right time and be very lucky. Those who claim to have witnessed something strange include boxer Mohammed Ali, film star Shirley MacLaine, rock musician John Lennon, the astronomer who discovered the planet Pluto, Dr. Clyde Tombaugh, and many more. But perhaps the most famous person to report a sighting is Jimmy Carter, who later became president of the United States.

The date was January 6, 1969. Carter was governor of the state of Georgia. He was standing outside the Lions Club in Leary, Georgia, preparing to give an address at 7:30 that evening, when the object appeared in the western sky amid a mass of twinkling stars. Ten other club members were with him and they all saw it too.

Jimmy Carter says that the object was like a big star, "about the same size as the moon, maybe a little smaller. It varied from brighter [and] larger than a planet to the apparent size of the moon."

At first the big round mass was stationary in the sky and colored blue, but as they watched, it began to rush towards the startled men, swinging back and forth like a pendulum and turning a deep red. The future president noted that it was "luminous [but] not solid." He had no idea what it was.

After about 10 minutes, the strange object seemed to move away backwards at a tangent from their position without moving across the sky, causing it to shrink in size. It was never seen again.

Carter did not report the incident until 1973, three years before he ascended to the White House. One of the other witnesses has since come forward to support him. That man is Fred Hart, who in 1969 was the president of the Lions Club, where Governor Carter was guest speaker. However, he does not seem to have been too excited by the odd light in the sky.

According to UFO skeptic Robert Shaeffer,

Jimmy Carter did not see a real flying saucer at all. He has calculated that the planet Venus was in just the right part of the sky that night and that this must have been what the men saw.

It's true that UFO investigators believe that as many as nine out of every ten sightings reported to be UFOs turn out to be IFOs, or *identified* flying objects. But why should it appear so strange to Carter and these other men? Carter was a trained scientist with a university degree in nuclear physics. He had served with the U.S. Navy. Surely he could be expected to recognize a planet such as Venus, which is a common sight in the evening and morning sky whenever it comes close to the earth!

What may have happened in January 1969 is that Venus was shining through a patch of sky that had unusual optical properties. These are known to produce mirages—just as in a hot desert you think you're seeing a pool of water ahead that is not really there. The rays of light from the planet would have been bent on their way towards the earth and magnified in size, causing just the sort of effect that Jimmy Carter reported.

Whether this particular UFO was an IFO or was indeed something else may be less important than the effect that it had on the beliefs of Jimmy Carter. When he became president in 1976, he pledged to do all he could to tell the truth about UFOs to the public that elected him. He went on record as saying, "I am convinced that UFOs exist. I have seen one."

Danger On the Highway

As we have already seen, some UFO encounters can be harmful to your health. The story of a restaurant owner, Betty Cash, shows how real that danger can be.

Betty and her friend and employee Vickie Landrum set off on the evening of December 29, 1980 towards Dayton, Texas. With them was Vickie's seven-year-old grandson, Colby. Betty wanted to check out a new restaurant and decided to make a social evening of it.

At around 9 P.M. they were driving home through a pine forest when a fiery object appeared in the sky ahead of them. It quickly descended to treetop height and hovered menacingly over the road blocking their path. They stopped the car just 135 feet (40.5 m) away.

Their descriptions of the object, as given later, varied. Betty said it looked like a very bright light with no obvious shape. Vickie thought it was long with a rounded top and pointed lower half. Colby said it reminded him of a huge diamond.

Even though they were afraid, the witnesses climbed out of the car for a better look. Bursts of flame jetted down from beneath the object, accompanied by sounds like a flame thrower. Throughout the encounter they heard a roaring and bleeping sound.

It was too much for Colby, who was very distressed. Vickie got back in the car with him. Betty remained looking at the object for a while longer. When she took hold of the door handle to join the other two, it was so hot it was difficult to grasp. The heat from the UFO was fierce now and burned her wedding ring into her finger. By now Colby was hysterical and his grandmother thought the end of the world had come.

Suddenly the object began to move off, and Betty decided to follow it. As she did, they noticed 23 twin rotor helicopters coming their way. These were later identified as Chinooks—military helicopters. They were either *chasing* or *escorting* the object away.

After stopping a few more times to watch the spectacle, the three went home. Betty arrived at 9:50 P.M., after first dropping off the others.

Within hours all three became ill.

Young Colby had a "sunburn" on his face and his eyes puffed up. Vickie also had swollen eyes and some of her hair fell out. Her boss, who had stayed outside the longest, suffered the most.

In the first four days Betty complained of blinding headaches and being sick. There were also neck pains, sore eyes and blisters on her scalp. She was admitted to Parkway General Hospital in Houston as a burn victim. Her symptoms were similar to radiation exposure, but none of the doctors could say for sure. She left the hospital, but soon had to return since she wasn't getting better. Her hair began falling out in clumps and she developed cancer.

All three victims were advised to sue the American government for compensation. If UFOs did not exist, as the American government publicly claimed, then the object had to be a new secret aircraft. If that was the case, then the government had failed to protect three of its citizens from the aircraft's damaging effects.

They decided to sue for $20 million. The case dragged on for several years in the U.S. District Court in Houston and attracted a lot of attention from the media. In court were representatives from NASA (the National Aeronautics and Space Administration), the U.S. Air Force, Army and Navy. The judge dismissed the case in 1986 on the grounds that no such object was owned, operated or listed by any department of the American government.

Two NASA scientists, John Shuessler and Dr.

Alan Holt investigated the case as part-time UFO researchers. They were very unhappy with the judge's decision. By accepting the "expert testimony," Judge Ross Sterling did not have to meet Betty Cash, Vickie Landrum and Colby Landrum. Also, the evidence of the Chinook helicopters was virtually ignored by the court, even though other people had come forward who also claimed to have seen them that night.

What then exactly did happen to Betty, Vickie and Colby? Rumors spread that the object was a nuclear-powered space shuttle that was not working properly, or that it was a captured alien spacecraft that the military were trying to fly.

If either of these explanations are right, then the helicopters were protecting and trying to escort the object away. But if it was "not of this world" and piloted by non-human beings, the Chinooks were chasing it. Either way the government and the court conspired in a major cover-up.

2. CLOSE ENCOUNTERS OF THE SECOND KIND— PHYSICAL EVIDENCE

- Desert touchdown—and real proof . . .

- UFOs can be hot property!

- UFO evidence captured by French scientists . . .

- If you meet a UFO in the forest—run!

Landing at Socorro

Police officer Lonnie Zamora was going about his usual routine on April 24, 1964, near the town of Socorro, New Mexico. Suddenly a speeding car raced by and he decided to give chase. It was a shiny new black Chevrolet. As he followed it towards the rodeo grounds, Zamora's attention was diverted by a loud roar and a bluish orange flame in the sky.

The officer concluded that a dynamite shack has exploded, and decided to investigate the "accident." He knew there was a shack in that area, but the flame was very peculiar. Zamora described it as "motionless, slowly descending, like a funnel—narrower at the top than the bottom." The noise was definitely a "roar," not a blast, and it was unlike the noise made by a jet aircraft. After about ten seconds, it changed from high to low frequency, and then stopped.

Zamora continued towards where the flame had disappeared behind a hill. The track up the hill was made of gravel and he made several attempts to drive over it. Steering carefully along the rough track, both windows wound down, he looked for the supposed dynamite shack. At last he reached the top of the hill.

Between 100 and 200 yards (100–200 m) away in a gully was a shiny object. He thought at first it was a car that had turned over. There were two "people" nearby in white coveralls. They looked like small adults or children. One of them stared at Zamora, obviously startled. The officer started driving towards them. As he drew closer, he assumed he was looking at a white vehicle standing on its radiator or trunk.

He radioed the sheriff's office, reported a possible automobile accident, and then stopped the car. While he was getting out, he dropped the microphone and stooped to pick it up. At this point, he heard three loud thumps, like someone closing a car door. Then the roar sounded again—only much nearer. It started off very low and rose in pitch. He looked up and saw a flame beneath the object that was now rising into the air. There was no smoke, just swirling dust.

Zamora now had a better look at the strange craft. It was oval-shaped and metallic, like aluminum. There were no doors or windows, but an unusual red insignia was marked on it.

Alarmed by all this, Zamora ducked behind the rise of the hill to protect himself, thinking the object was about to explode. He intended to keep on running, but instead turned in time to see it fly off, missing the dynamite shack by just three feet (1 m). As it flew away he came back to the car and radioed the sheriff's office again to update his report. There was no sign of the small "men."

He asked the radio operator, Ned Lopez, to "look out of the window to see if you can see the object." But Zamora did not tell him *which* window so he probably looked in the wrong direction. Zamora watched as the object cleared the Six Mile Canyon Mountains and disappeared from sight.

Sergeant Chavez was first on the scene, followed by Deputy James Lucky. He called Captain Richard Holder, in charge of the tracking station of the White Sands Missile Base located to the south of Socorro.

At the landing site four clear impressions were found in the sand. These "landing marks" were later photographed. Marks resembling footprints were also discovered nearby. There was also some brush burning.

Later FBI agent Arthur Byrnes took a detailed report from Zamora. One of the investigators was Dr. Allen Hynek, who was then working for the U.S. Air Force investigating UFO reports. He concluded that Zamora was telling the truth—that he saw what he said he saw.

Three local people also reported to the police that they had seen the strange flame in the sky. There were also two witnesses who called in at a service station and told the attendant that they had seen a strange craft flying low over Highway 85. They were later identified as Paul Kies and Larry Kratzer of Dubuque, Iowa.

Major Hector Quintanilla, head of "Project Blue Book"—the title given to the Air Force investigation of UFOs—had initially thought the object was an experimental craft belonging to NASA, but that proved not to be the answer. He said: "This was probably the best-documented case in the Air Force files and I've checked it out everywhere."

The case remains in official files as UNIDENTIFIED.

Burned at Falcon Lake

Steve Michalak was a 52-year-old industrial mechanic whose hobby was geology. On May 20, 1967, he was prospecting around Falcon Lake, 80 miles east of Winnipeg, near the Trans Canada Highway.

Just after he ate lunch, his attention was drawn to some geese cackling on a nearby swamp. There were two scarlet lights above in the clear sky. They began to descend and Steve could see that they were cigar-shaped objects with a hump on top. While one hovered over some trees, the other landed about 130 feet (43 m) away. Suddenly, the hovering craft sped off into the sky.

The landed craft then changed color from scarlet to grey-red to grey and finally silver. The same effect takes place when hot metal cools down. Steve could see now that the craft was disc-shaped, about 35 feet (11 m) in diameter, with a dome on top and nine vent-like openings around its sloping sides. Each contained about 30 small holes set in a grille. There were also a continuous whistling of air and a whining sound.

Steve stalked the silent object and made some sketches. He observed it for half an hour through the welding goggles that he usually wore to protect his eyes from rock chips. As he sketched, Steve felt waves of heat coming from the craft, along with a vile stench like sulphur. Then a doorway appeared in the side, and a brilliant violet beam shone out. It was bright enough to light up the ground in sunlight. He saw no one, but heard voices inside speaking in a language he did not recognize.

Gaining confidence, Steve approached the craft. There were no welding and no joints, and the surface of the object was highly polished. He looked inside. Small lights were flashing randomly. Convinced now that he was dealing with a secret experimental aircraft, he tried to communicate with whoever was inside, speaking in several languages, but the only reply was the sudden closing of the door. He stepped back, but nothing else happened, so he came nearer again.

As he did, he placed his gloved hand on the shiny surface.

This was a mistake—the glove melted! At that instant the craft tilted slightly upwards and a blast of heat hit him from one of the vents. It sent him reeling and set his shirt on fire. Steve tore his shirt off and saw the craft disappear over some trees.

A tremendously strong odor of sulphur hung over the swamp, and waves of nausea swept over Steve. He gathered up his things and began the two-mile (3 km) trek to the highway. Along the route he vomited an estimated 200 times. It took him two hours to go the two miles. On the highway he flagged down a police patrol car. The officer listened to his story, but explained he had other duties to perform and left him stranded! Eventually a motorist picked him up. Returning to Winnipeg, Steve was immediately admitted to a hospital.

This was the start of the treatment for a mysterious illness that was to plague him for a year and a half. During his illness he was examined by 27 doctors and ran up huge medical bills. After treatment for first-degree burns, the hospital released him. He had lost a great deal of weight and a rash appeared on his chest. Nausea and mental blackouts were continual during this time. During August 1968, the pattern of a grille appeared on his chest.

He was tested for radiation contamination by the Whiteshell Nuclear Research Establishment, but only normal levels were found. However, Dr. Horace Dudley, former chief of the Radio-isotope Laboratory, U.S. Naval Hospital, New York, believed that Michalak's symptoms were "a classic picture of severe whole body exposure to radiation."

Radioactivity *was* found at the landing site with fragments of metal, mostly silver, that had been exposed to great heat. Investigations were conducted by the Department of Health and Welfare and National Defence, the National Research Council, the University of Colorado and the Canadian Aerial Phenomena Research Organisation.

The Defence Minister refused to make public the findings of his government departments. After much persistence, a file on the case was presented in the Canadian House of Commons. UFOlogist Arthur Bray who had seen the original compiled by the National Research Council, examined this version and claimed that important data had been left out.

Skeptics tried to prove that Steve Michalak had made the whole thing up, and had deliberately burned himself with a red-hot barbecue grille to provide "evidence." Many others, however, believe that he was telling the truth.

Not of This Earth

Renato Nicolai was lucky. He owned land astride a beautiful valley in the south of France near the village of Trans-en-Provence. From his home he could stare out over the terraced hillsides that sloped towards the river and lazily watch the sun sink down into the rich tapestry of croplands.

However, this area hid a secret that few farmers wished to discuss. A local peak at Draguinan, called La Malmont (literally meaning "the evil mountain"), had for years generated strange lights and terrifying apparitions of mysterious dark figures. Other witnesses had seen alien entities and met forces that stalled car engines for no apparent reason.

But something was lacking from all of these reports—physical proof. Unexpectedly, Renato Nicolai was about to offer that evidence to the French government, who would spend several years pondering what to do with it.

It was around 5 P.M. on January 8, 1981. The farmer was attracted by a strange humming or whistling noise as he worked at the rear of his yard. The noise was coming from above, so he glanced upwards, just in time to catch sight of a bizarre object at treetop height descending onto one of the carefully layered terraces at the back of his steeply sloping land.

The thing was only a few feet in diameter. It was oval in shape and grey in color, and on the underside were small legs set into the base. It was falling slowly and purposefully toward a landing and Nicolai marched off towards it, curious about what it could be.

He never got close enough to touch the object. As he approached the device the constant high-pitched whistle rose to a crescendo and the thing climbed skywards, accelerating rapidly. Then it turned in flight towards a horizontal mode and shot away across the sky into the darkening clouds.

Renato did not want to make a fuss, but told a neighbor about the experience. That man called the police, who arrived probably expecting to hear another tall tale from a wine-swilling local.

Instead, they were greeted by a very sober man and shown the spot where the thing had come down.

In France the police—or *gendarmerie*, as they are called—have a unique function. In 1977 the French government set up a UFO investigation team at the national space center in Toulouse. Gendarmerie officers are trained to carry out studies of reported sightings and call the scientists if they seem to be important. Research laboratories all over the country are on alert to assess any physical evidence that might prove UFOs a reality.

The gendarmerie quickly concluded that the landing at Trans-en-Provence had no explanation and might offer such proof. They took samples of soil from the affected area and sent them to Toulouse. Soon afterwards, scientists were winging their way across the country to this little farming hamlet, ready to be convinced that it was the scene of an extraordinary close encounter.

Renato was investigated by a psychologist, who was satisfied that he was telling the truth. Three laboratories also took samples of the soil and plants from where the UFO touched the earth and control samples from a local terrace far from where the UFO had landed. These brought some astonishing results.

They found that the ground had been crushed from above and heated to a temperature between 300° and 600° C (572° to 1112° F). But they could not tell what force had made this happen. Unusual levels of some chemicals, such as zinc, were found only in the landing area—not outside it.

Professor Michel Bounais from the National Institute of Agricultural Research then found even more impressive evidence. Chlorophyll, a vital chemical in plants and leaves, had been reduced by up to 50 percent inside the landing ring. Outside of it there was nothing abnormal.

Possibly as significant was the finding that the variations in the levels of chlorophyll showed a precise mathematical relationship. The further from the center point of the landing ring, the more chlorophyll was found in the samples. This suggests that the damage was caused by the thing that descended from above and left its mark on the farmer's hillside.

Over the years since 1981 Renato Nicolai's land has gradually returned to normal, but no answer has been found as to what strange power caused the dramatic physical evidence at this site.

Various scientists have visited the spot to try to solve the mystery and left completely baffled. But evidently something touched down upon the slopes and changed the crops that lay beneath in a quite remarkable manner.

Many researchers now believe that it was something not of this earth.

If You Go Down to the Woods Today

Bob Taylor loved the forest. It was his job and his hobby. This morning he was on a routine trek to inspect the trees and make sure that everything was fine. He had been on duty since 7:30 A.M., but his home was not too far away and he could return there if necessary.

His dog always went with him, just in case he should meet unwelcome intruders. But an inconceivable danger was lurking in the forest.

It was a typically crisp Scottish morning in mid-autumn, November 9, 1979. Bob had parked his pickup truck at the edge of a slightly muddy track and proceeded on foot. Although close by the main freeway that links Edinburgh with Glasgow and astride the fast-growing town of Livingston, this area had little traffic. Nobody else was likely to see whatever took place within these shadowy woodlands.

Rounding a bend and approaching a clearing, Bob came upon the weirdest object he had ever seen, hovering just above the grass. Shaped rather like the planet Saturn, it was essentially rounded, with a flat rim across the middle. Some tiny windmill-like arms were located on a central band. There were also a few small windows. Bob could not see around the back, but the rim seemed to encircle the craft completely, implying that it was spherical. It was not much bigger than a medium-sized car.

However, there was something sinister about it. The color was greyish but not consistent. It faded in and out in an odd way and shrubbery behind it became visible through its body. It was as if this giant sphere were trying to camouflage itself but not quite pulling it off.

Bob Taylor watched intently, fear submerged in wonder, as the object blinked in and out of reality. Then two monsters came from behind the craft and headed straight towards the woodsman. He was under attack with nowhere to run.

They were not human, not even alien. In fact, they resembled sea urchins (mines)—round balls a foot or so (.3 m) in diameter and covered with spikes. They bounced along the wet ground, making a terrible sucking noise. Later Bob realized that this sound was probably the spikes embedding themselves in the damp soil.

The two weird things moved apart and went to either side of the forester. Before he had a chance to react, there was a strange smell. He experienced a sickening feeling, a burning in his throat and the sensation of being grabbed by the side of the legs and tugged forward. Then there was just blackness. Bob Taylor had plunged into unconsciousness.

The 61-year-old man came to with the sound of barking in his ears. His dog was racing around the little clearing, snarling and yapping in anger and frustration.

The woodsman's head was pounding. He was woozy; his throat was sore and he could not even scream for help. As he tried to stand he collapsed onto his knees, still with a bitter, dry taste in his mouth.

Bob had no idea how much time had passed, but it still seemed to be mid-morning. Later estimates suggested he was unconscious for about 20 minutes. He could see neither the craft nor the monsters. Had his dog frightened them away?

Bob crawled painfully towards his truck, his trusty dog trailing anxiously behind. He scrambled into the cab and jerked it into gear, but his coordination was awry and he succeeded only in driving into a muddy ditch and getting stuck there.

Stumbling out, Bob slowly scrambled towards his house on the edge of the woods. He just had to get away from there. That machine might come back.

When Bob staggered into his house, his wife saw at once that he had been attacked. His hair was matted and he was splattered with mud. A doctor called on Bob at about noon, although by then he was recovering well. However, the practitioner still insisted that the woodsman visit the hospital. Bob Taylor reluctantly agreed.

In the forest, the police cordoned off the site. They had found evidence to back up Bob's story. On the ground at the spot where he had directed them to look there was a series of flattened marks and indented holes. These were consistent with the traces that would have been left by the craft and the weird spiked objects that had emerged from it.

The local police department treated this case as a serious assault by person or persons unknown. This remains the only time in British history that a UFO encounter was subjected to a criminal investigation.

The media were soon swarming around the forest, but were prevented from inspecting the trace marks. Bob signed himself out of the hospital feeling better. He and his wife went south to England to visit relatives, as they had planned to do before the nightmare took place. This prompted incorrect media reports that Bob had fled the country in terror.

The press interest soon vanished, but UFOlogists and police pursued the story for many months. Bob Taylor's trousers were given a forensic examination and showed tear marks that were the product of a downward force. This certainly supported his claims about what had happened. The UFOlogists, using tiny samples of different gases, identified the smell that Bob had reported during his attack as being sulfur dioxide.

Bob Taylor made no money from his story and shunned most offers of publicity. He soon retired and moved away to avoid the constant attention.

As for the townsfolk of Livingston, they came to be proud of their very own close encounter. In 1992 a small plaque and cairn of stones was erected in the woodlands proclaiming what had happened there in 1979.

A few weeks after the ceremony, the plaque vanished in the middle of the night and was never seen again. Perhaps it is now the centerpiece of a private museum somewhere on earth—or indeed, somewhere off it!

3. CLOSE ENCOUNTERS OF THE THIRD KIND— ALIEN CONTACT

- Sightings in Russia . . .
- Goblins from the stars lay siege to a farm . . .
- The first portrait of an alien . . .
- Horror on a lonely highway as a UFO takes control of a family's car . . .

Invasion at Voronezh

It happened in the industrial city of Voronezh, some 300 miles southeast of Moscow, in Russia. On October 9, 1989, the news agency Tass announced that there had been several UFO encounters around the city. The story was big news. Previously, the Soviet Union would never have admitted that such a thing had happened.

Many of the witnesses were children. The case was investigated by Soviet UFOlogist Vladimir Lebedev and Dr. Henry Silanov, Director of the Spectral Department of the Voronezh

Geological-Geophysical Laboratory. Dr. Silanov provided the authors with the following report and eyewitness statements.

"In the period between September 21 to October 28, 1989, in the Western Park, six landings and one sighting (hovering) were registered, with the appearance of walking beings. We have collected a wealth of video materials with eyewitness accounts, particularly from pupils of the nearest school. We have no doubts they are telling the truth."

Vasya Surin was one of the students. He and his friends watched as a red sphere appeared out of a pink fog and some entities and robot-like creatures came out of it.

Several young witnesses signed statements on another incident, which took place at about 2:30 on the afternoon of October 28. Vova Startsev was playing hooky from school with his friends when they also saw a large pink sphere, flying.

"It was pink," Vova said, "but kept changing shades. On the left-hand side of the body were two antennae. It pushed out four legs, a hatch opened, a ladder came down and two beings and a robot came out. They carried the robot, set him on his feet and gave him artificial respiration. Then he walked like a man. He came up to me followed by one of the extraterrestrials. He was just under two metres (6 feet) tall. He stretched out his hand towards me, but I ran towards a tree and climbed it, shaking with fear. The alien had a big head, twice as big as ours, and three eyes in a row."

Vova was joined by one of his friends, Sergei Makarov, who added that the aliens wore silver suits, silver waistcoats with silver buttons and boots. Their faces were the color of "grilled beef-burgers," but their skin was smooth. When the door opened in the object, a blinding light shone out. As the students watched, the legs retracted into the object. Then it hovered before rising and flying off.

Was this same object seen earlier, towards the end of September? Denis Valyerervich Murzenko had changed his clothes to go to a concert with his mother. He decided to go for a walk while she was getting ready. Looking up into the sky he saw something pink, shaped like an egg, with rays of light coming from it. The object came closer and began to swing from side to side like a falling leaf. At this point two supports came out from underneath. Denis could see the outline of someone inside the object.

"The 'person' seemed to be about four and a half feet (1.2 m) high, with an old face. I stood still and it kept coming down lower and lower. I got frightened and ran off. When I turned I saw bright beams of light. The object stopped next to the flagstones. There was some kind of sound like music."

Several days later Denis noticed a suspicious man hanging around at the location of the UFO landing. There was a metal plate on his chest with some markings on it.

"He stood for a while, got on his knees, touched the grass and then started to wave his arms about. Then he got up, ran off, and then walked normally. I followed him and he went into a shed. I was only 20 metres (60 feet) behind him, but when I arrived, he had gone."

There were many more accounts from other witnesses. It was clear that something very strange had occurred—the stories were too similar to be made up. But what had happened exactly? Dr. Silanov, who examined the landing site, said in his report that tests "registered incredibly high levels of magnetism. It is evident that something produced it." Imprints in the ground were also measured. These were made, it was concluded, by an object weighing around eleven tons.

Siege at Sutton Farm

Kelly is a hamlet a few miles north of Hopkinsville, Kentucky. On the night of August 21, 1955, one of the most amazing cases of alien contact took place there. Eight adults and three children at the Sutton Farm witnessed it.

It began at 7:00 P.M., when Billy Ray Taylor, a friend of the Sutton family, went out to the well for some water. As he was taking a drink he saw a huge shining object land in a dried-up riverbed close to the farm. He ran inside and told the others. They laughed, thinking he had seen something ordinary, like a shooting star. Less than an hour later, they were alerted by the furious barking of their dog in the yard. This usually happened when strangers visited the farm.

Lucky Sutton, the eldest son and head of the house since the death of his stepfather, went with Billy to investigate. They were absolutely amazed at what they saw. Walking towards the farm was a figure with its arms in the air as if in surrender. More bizarre than this, the figure was not human.

Shining, as if illuminated from inside, it was just over three-feet (1 m) tall with a bald egg-shaped head. The eyes were yellow and big as saucers. The mouth was a large gash stretching between elephant-like ears. Its short legs were thin and its long arms ended in claws.

Thinking along the lines of "Shoot first, ask questions later," the men let loose at the being with a shotgun and a .22 rifle. It was only about seven yards (6.3 m) from the house when they fired, so there was no chance of missing. The men described the sound as "exactly as if you had shot into a pail." The visitor somersaulted backwards and scurried away into the darkness.

This was the start of several hours of terror.

Other identical creatures converged on the farm from all sides. They peered through the windows at the terrified, gun-happy occupants and were only scared away when fired at or when an outside light was switched on. Light seemed to have a worse effect than bullets.

The creatures uttered no sound when they

were shot, and although the undergrowth crackled as they walked through it, there was never any sound of footsteps. All the beings approached the house with arms raised, as if expressing peaceful intent. Once shot at, however, their arms dropped and they would scurry off on all fours. The entities never tried to force any entry into the house nor attack the occupants.

After the first shooting, another—or the same—creature appeared at a window. The men fired, causing it to flip backwards. Thinking they had disabled it, they decided to creep outside for a look. The women urged them not to shoot anymore, since the beings had not acted in a hostile manner. As Billy stepped outside, a silvery hand reached down from the low-hanging roof and brushed his hair. Those still inside saw this and dragged him back. Lucky rushed outside and fired a volley of shots at point-blank range, knocking the entity from the roof. Interestingly, even though the creature could have harmed Billy with its sharp talons, it had not.

Another creature was hanging in the branches of a nearby maple tree. Both men fired at this one and it *floated* to the ground and scurried off. Another came around the side of the house, and they shot that one too, with the same negative effect. Understandably concerned that their weapons were useless against the invaders, the men ran back inside to decide what to do next.

Glennie Lankford, the mother of the family, ordered the men to end their hostility towards the creatures. The entities kept peering through the windows, however, and the three children became hysterical. It was now 11 P.M. They decided to make a run for it. The family piled into two cars and headed at top speed to the Hopkinsville police station.

The police returned with the family and searched the farm. Although there was evidence of gunfire, there was little else, aside from a luminous patch of ground where one of the creatures had fallen when it was shot. At 2:15 A.M. the searchers left, leaving the family alone at the farm.

They felt reassured enough to go to bed. Glennie Lankford was lying awake, watching the window, when she noticed a luminous glow coming through it. It was one of the creatures staring in at her. She calmly called the rest of the family, and despite her protestations, Lucky shot at the being, to no effect. The siege continued until just before sunrise.

Later that day, once again on the way to the Sutton Farm, police officers saw several bright lights coming from that direction. But when they made a thorough search, they could find no physical proof of the reality of the creatures. A neighbor, however, did notice some strange lights in a field at the time the entities were said to have been making for the farm building.

Could the Suttons have fabricated the entire incident and carried it through so perfectly? Or did UFO entities actually terrorize the family at Kelly?

The Alien on Ilkley Moor

A former British police officer had an unsettling experience on December 1, 1987. Philip Spencer lived in Ilkley at the time, a village in the Yorkshire moors.

At 7:15 A.M. Philip said goodbye to his wife and children and set off across Ilkley Moor to visit his father-in-law, who lived in a village on the other side. It was still dark when he began his journey, but he carried his camera with him, hoping to take some photographs of Ilkley from the moor tops as dawn broke.

In an area known as White Wells, something caught his attention. Philip was passing a small

19th century quarry cut into the hilltop when a movement made him look around. There, just ten feet (1 m) away, was "a small green creature." Instinctively, he brought his camera up, but the creature shuffled away and then stopped again. It turned to him and made a dismissive movement with its right arm. Without checking the camera setting, Philip only had time to take one photograph before the entity disappeared behind an outcropping.

Philip later described the creature to investigators. It was about 4 feet 6 inches (1.35 m) tall with large pointed ears, big black eyes, no nose and a small mouth. Its arms were very long, with enormous hands. Its feet were cloven, and it was covered with rough-looking green skin.

The instant the creature disappeared, Philip ran into the quarry and followed it around the outcropping. There a bigger shock awaited him. The entity had disappeared, but hovering before him was a silver saucer-shaped object. It was like two cereal bowls stuck together. In a split second it rose into the sky and vanished.

Somewhat bewildered, Philip returned to Ilkley. There he glanced at the church clock and saw it was 10 A.M. Almost two hours had been lost from his life! He began to wonder if he had been hallucinating, and took his camera film to be processed. He was both relieved and disturbed when he collected the film an hour later. Although the photograph was underexposed and slightly blurred, it showed the creature, and proved he had not imagined the encounter.

The negative was latter examined by Kodak, who said it had not been tampered with. What appeared in the picture had really been there.

Philip began having strange dreams. In the dreams he saw a pattern of stars in the sky. They worried him. He wondered what had happened during the missing time. UFO investigators introduced him to a clinical psychologist who agreed to hypnotize him and make him relive the close encounter. Of course, since hypnosis is not a truth drug, no one knows for sure how much imagination might color a real memory.

Nevertheless, the hypnosis session came up with some surprises—not least of which was the revelation that Philip had been approached by the creature *before* he took the photograph! Here are Philip's actual words under hypnosis:

"I'm walking along the moor. Oh! It's quite windy. There's a lot of clouds. Walking up towards the trees, I see this little something, can't tell, but he's green. It's moving towards me. Oh! I can't move, I'm stuck! He's still coming towards me. And I still can't move. . . . I'm stuck, and everything's gone fuzzy. I'm . . . I'm floating along in the air. . . . I want to get down! And this green thing's walking ahead of me, and I don't like it.

"I still can't move. I'm going around the corner and this green thing's in front of me. *Oh, God, I want to get down.* There's a . . . there's a big silver saucer thing, and there's a door in it, and I don't want to go in there! Everything's gone black now. . . ."

Philip described a medical examination inside the object by several of the green creatures. Afterwards he was taken on a tour and shown a "movie." It was an ecological warning of what would happen to our world if we do not curb pollution and control population growth.

Afterwards, Philip was put back on the moors with no conscious memory of what had occurred.

The investigation of the case involved scientists from the University of Manchester as well as UFOlogists, including Peter Hough and Jenny Randles of the Manchester UFO Research Association, photograph experts and the clinical psychologist.

Some people believe the case is a hoax, although no proof was found for this. The witness never sought to make any money, even though it was offered, and insisted that his true identity be kept secret. Jim Singleton, the psychologist, commented:

"Philip was certainly recounting the incident as something which had actually happened. He described things typically as someone would recall a past event. He compares very well with other non-UFO subjects."

Until evidence has been uncovered to resolve the case one way or another, this will remain one of the most perplexing UFO incidents on record. Philip is one of the very few abductees who apparently managed to take a photograph of one of his abductors.

Hijacked by a UFO

Faye Knowles shifted her position in the car and watched the dark road unwind ahead. It had been a long journey and there were hundreds of miles still to go.

She had packed her three adult sons into the car, bundled in the family dog, and left Perth the day before. They had set off on the 2,000 mile (3,219 km) trek heading for South Australia to visit distant relatives.

It was now after 4 A.M. on January 20, 1988 and a time of great celebration. Australia was just 200 years old as a settlement and there were big parties and spectacular events happening all over the country. But at this hour of the morning there was little traffic on the Eyre Highway, a ribbon of road in a long, straight line dividing sea from searing desert.

The vast brooding plains of the Nullarbor were invisible in the darkness, but they had left their mark. In the southern hemisphere it was high summer and journeys of any length in this region were best contemplated at night when it was much cooler.

The only other vehicles on the road were two trucks, one in front and one some miles behind the Knowles family. They were in radio contact with each other, the drivers being friends who made long distance runs quite often.

Suddenly, ahead of the Knowles car, looming on the eastern horizon, was a strange light. It was pale yellow and seemed to be jerking around from side to side not unlike a swirling whirlwind.

"What's that?" came from the back seat, merely curious at first. But curiosity soon turned into fear. The thing headed straight at them! Zigzagging from side to side, it hovered in front of the car like an avenging angel. It resembled an egg in an egg cup—an oval balloon on top of a tapering column reaching down to the ground.

One minute the thing was about to hit them, the next it was behind them and receding at great speed. Panic rose in the voices of the travellers. Even the dog was growing nervous, shuffling about and whimpering.

Nightmare minutes followed as the object twisted and turned. They lost sight of it for a while, but then the thing came back at them from the other direction. In one moment of terror, Faye's son who was driving the car swerved around at high speed and reversed course. He was desperate to get away. There seemed to be no escape from the thing.

At one point, as they weaved across the road, a car towing a trailer came flashing out of the darkness straight at them. They managed to drag themselves out of its path, narrowly avoiding a disastrous collision.

The UFO was now above them and invisible, but they could all hear a high-pitched humming coming from overhead. The car was being buffeted, as if by high winds, and a terrible smell—pungent electrical burning—was filling the car along with a faint grey mist.

Faye Knowles had her passenger window open, trying to see what was going on. She couldn't see anything, but she could certainly feel it. Her fingers touched the car roof and met something strange. It felt soft and spongy. Immediately, she yanked her hand back in and shut the window.

But now something even more horrific was taking place. The car was being sucked up off the roadway. The thing above them was acting like a huge vacuum cleaner, pulling them upwards as they tried to fight it off.

The wheels spun around without taking them forward. They were floating several feet in the air, while still being propelled ahead in some way! The Knowles family were no longer in control of the car—*it* was!

These moments of fear seemed to last forever. Yet, even as they cried out, there was another weird effect. Their voices seemed distorted and twisted. They sounded to each other like cartoon characters. They had never experienced anything like it before.

Then, as quickly as the terrible events had started, they came to an end. The car crashed down onto the road again, and they slewed across, blindly unaware whether or not any traffic was coming in the other direction. If it had been, they would have smashed into it head-on.

They crashed off the edge of the highway into scrub bush and screamed to a halt, one tire reduced to shreds and the car studded with dust and impact damage from small stones.

For many minutes they sat still in the quiet night, breathing heavily and regaining composure. After a while, the four of them got out and replaced the damaged tire, still watching the sky and keeping an eye out for the UFO. They knew it was out there—in the distance—waiting.

As soon as they were able, the Knowles family piled back into the car and shot back onto the road. They drove east, putting as many miles as possible between themselves and the object. Thankfully, they never saw it again.

A half hour later, as the sun rose, they pulled

into the small town of Mundrabilla. Here they told their story to the owners of a roadside diner, who could see the shock etched onto the faces of the "hijacked" family. The truck drivers were also in town and one of them had briefly seen the UFO.

Inside the battered car there was a fine sprinkling of powder or dust and a faint musty smell. On the roof, where Faye Knowles said that she had felt something spongy that seemed to be tugging them upwards, were four indentations about the size of a fist.

Later that morning the family stopped at a police station to report the incident. Both police and UFO investigators took samples of the powder from the car, but laboratory tests could not reach a firm conclusion. However, one group of investigators said that they found traces of the same chemicals used by NASA in the design of the space shuttle. These chemicals coat the surface as a protection against great heat on re-entry.

Other people on the road that night described how their cars were hit by terrific blasts of wind that struck out of nowhere. This led to the theory by a professor from Adelaide University that the UFO had really been a fierce and very unusual form of electrically charged tornado.

Of course, other people had different ideas. Many felt sure that the Knowles family had had a very narrow escape at the hands of an alien craft, one that had been intent on snatching the unsuspecting family and taking them away.

4. CLOSE ENCOUNTERS OF THE FOURTH KIND— ABDUCTED!

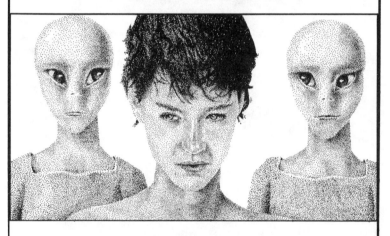

- A couple gets taken for a ride— in space . . .

- A woodsman is captured by aliens in front of witnesses . . .

- One of our aircraft is missing . . .

- Space flight over Manhattan!

Spacenapped!

Betty and Barney Hill claim to be the first Americans to be abducted by aliens and taken inside their flying craft. They were victims of what is now called "spacenapping."

Betty was a welfare worker and Barney was an employee of the post office in Portsmouth, New Hampshire. During September 1961, they had been on vacation in Canada, touring around Niagara Falls. After a happy few days away from home, they were taking the long drive back through the White Mountains.

Suddenly they became aware of a light—like a big star—that seemed to be following them as they drove the twisting highway. They tried to figure out what it might be—a helicopter or aircraft? But as long as the white light stayed high in the sky, it was just a curiosity.

Near Indian Head, the dancing ball swooped down much closer. Rather frightened by this change, they slowed the car and stopped. Barney got out to look at the thing through binoculars, noting how it resembled a banana with pointed ends and that it had windows in the middle. He then started to walk towards the hovering object as if in some kind of trance.

Betty Hill was frightened by her husband's odd behavior. Panicked, she cried out for him to return, but he didn't seem to hear her voice and kept walking into the darkly outlined trees.

Finally, Barney shook himself free of the compulsion that was pulling him into the woods and returned to the car. But he claimed to have seen faces in the windows. Alien creatures were inside the craft. That was enough for the two of them. They decided to get away from there as fast as they could.

As they drove away, they heard strange beeping sounds that went on for a few seconds, then stopped. They ignored them and rushed home. Only in the cold light of morning did they realize that their journey had taken longer than it should have. More than an hour of time had been stolen from their minds. The car also had some odd blotches on the hood.

Betty told her story to a local UFO investigator, who discovered that Pease Air Force Base, whose radar covers the Indian Head area, had tracked an unknown object in the middle of the night at about the same time that the Hills saw their flying banana. But the case was simply put on record and added to all of the others that were piling up.

Betty Hill started to have nightmares in which she saw strange white-skinned faces with large slanted eyes, narrow noses and slit-like mouths. Barney was suffering from anxiety and depression and was having trouble working. In the end they both sought medical help.

After consulting several doctors, they found their way to Dr. Benjamin Simon in Boston, who used hypnosis with his patients, taking them back over memories that disturbed them to relieve their stress.

Dr. Simon was astonished by what the couple described. Under hypnosis both husband and wife reacted in terror as they told of being taken by force into the banana-shaped UFO at the point where they had stopped their car. The beings were smaller than humans and seemed intent on studying their captives and finding out all about them.

Inside the UFO both Betty and Barney were given medical tests and samples of blood were taken from them. Some of these tests were unusual and hurt a little. The aliens seemed very puzzled by this pain.

Before they took the couple back to their car,

one of the aliens showed Betty something on the wall that had dots and lines on it. She was told that it was a map of the stars and the trading routes that the aliens travelled along in outer space. But she could not understand it unless she knew the correct position of the earth in the universe.

Betty tried to take something with her—a sort of alien book. She said that nobody would believe what had happened to her without some evidence. After some discussion the aliens decided that they could not let her take this away from the UFO.

In 1965 a famous New England writer, John Fuller, wrote their story into a book that was called *The Interrupted Journey*. It was a great success around the world and was later made into a TV movie called *The UFO Incident*.

Schoolteacher Marjorie Fish re-created the star map that Betty Hill recalled under hypnosis. Using her knowledge of astronomy, Fish tried to work out what the trading routes might be and which of the stars would then be home to the aliens. She concluded that they came from a planet that circled the star Zeta Reticulii, many light years from the earth.

When the strange story of the Hill spacenapping was told to the world, it was not unique. There had already been a similar case reported to UFOlogists in South America. A young Brazilian farmer had been spacenapped in October 1957 and reported it soon afterwards to a doctor. The incident had been investigated in January

1958 in Rio de Janeiro by scientists who filed a report with UFO investigators in England.

The English researchers had deliberately chosen not to publish the story, hoping that somebody else would report a similar case without knowing anything about the Brazilian events. The Hills did exactly that. The comparisons were very close and suggested that both stories might be more than just dreams. Betty and Barney Hill could not possibly have heard about the Brazilian farmer's claims when they reported seeing the UFO near Indian Head. These two amazing cases were completely isolated from one another.

This was vital evidence for UFOlogists, implying that spacenappings really were taking place. But if they were, the story told by Betty and Barney Hill was alarming. For it suggested that most people who had entered an alien spaceship might not remember it or ever know what had happened to them, except perhaps through dreams or under medical hypnosis. It might have happened to anyone—even you!

Fire in the Sky

Heber in Arizona was the location for a very different kind of UFO abduction that has since been made into a movie.

Mike Rogers and his crew of six forestry workers loaded their gear onto a truck and set off for home at about 6:15 P.M. on November 5, 1975. The had only travelled 100 yards (90 m) through the pine forest when crew member Alan Dalis pointed out a glow through the trees. At the top of a hill, they came to a clearing and the driver braked hard.

There, hovering about 20 feet (6 m) above a woodpile was a disc-shaped object. A framework divided it up into panels and it glowed amber. While the rest of the crew stared in fear and wonder, 22-year-old Travis Walton jumped out and moved towards the object. It began to wobble and make some very peculiar noises.

Suddenly a bright ray of greenish-blue light arrowed down from the disc and struck Walton about the head and shoulders. It flung him backwards. At this point, driver Mike Rogers panicked and drove the truck away at a fast speed on the rough logging road. After a quarter of a mile he stopped, and the men decided they had to go back and look for their friend. They returned but there was no trace of Walton or the object.

This was the start of a very strange story. It is extremely rare for anyone to observe a UFO abduction; it is even more peculiar for the abducted person to disappear for more than a couple of hours. Walton did not turn up until five days later.

In the meantime, there was a police investigation and a thorough search of the area. The story captured the imagination of the world. At one point the authorities thought the men had murdered their colleague and concocted the fantastic tale. Afterwards, it seemed there were only two possibilities: Walton had really been abducted by non-human beings, or the whole thing was a hoax.

Navajo County Sheriff's Deputy Chuck Ellison described the men as "extremely upset," and added: "If they were lying, they were damned good actors." One of the men was so affected he was weeping.

Allegedly, there were some initial polygraph tests carried out on the forestry workers that were not decisive. The so-called lie-detector test measures the stress generated by answers a person gives to specific questions. Later the crew passed tests given by Cy Gilson of the Arizona Department of Public Safety.

When Travis Walton called from a telephone booth a few miles outside of Heber at 11 P.M. on November 10, his brother-in-law and older brother, Duane, found him distraught and confused. He had an unbelievable story to tell the world.

He remembered being struck by the beam, which hit him like a bolt of electricity, then blackness. Next, he found himself in pain, lying on his back staring at a brightly lit ceiling, struggling into consciousness. Walton assumed he had been picked up off the forest floor and taken to a hospital. When he lifted his head and saw, instead of doctors and nurses, three non-human beings, he panicked and leaped off the table on which he had been lying.

The beings were about five feet (1.5m) tall with domed hairless heads, large eyes, tiny ears and nose, and a slit for a mouth. Walton grabbed a piece of equipment to use as a weapon, and the beings hurriedly left the room. Some minutes later, Walton followed them out into a corridor, but turned in the opposite direction. He entered another room that gave him an amazing view of the universe. Operating the controls set in a reclining chair, Walton found he could alter the perspective of billions of stars.

Suddenly, a being entered the planetarium. He looked human but wore a space helmet. He ignored Walton's questions and signalled him to follow. They stepped out of the object into a huge hangar that housed several other disc-shaped craft. He saw three more "humans"—two men and a woman. They all looked similar. They were six feet (1.8 m) tall with brownish-blond hair, golden eyes and tan-colored skin.

Once again Walton asked where he was and what had happened to him, but the questions were still ignored. Instead, the beings gestured to him to lie down. He did. One of them placed a mask over his face and the blackness returned.

He came to on the highway outside of Heber. A blast of heat hit his face from a disc hovering overhead, which then disappeared into the sky. He found a telephone and called his brother-in-law.

What really happened to Travis Walton? Was the whole thing a hoax that got out of hand, or were the men telling the truth? If it was a hoax, it is remarkable, as any police officer will verify, that in the intervening two decades not one of the perpetrators has hinted at the truth.

Did beings in an unidentified flying object really abduct Walton? If so, then *why?*

A Flight into Oblivion

Frederick Valentich loved flying. A young man, he could not afford his own plane, but had an agreement to use a Cessna from Moorabin Field in Melbourne, Australia. He often took it up to be at one with the clouds.

Frederick had another passion, less well known to his friends. He read all he could about flying saucers, even had a scrapbook of stories that he took with him on his trips. In October 1978, he was in his element because there was an ongoing wave of sightings above Bass Strait, between the mainland and the island of Tasmania.

On October 21, amid media reports of orange lights and cigar-shaped objects, Valentich planned to fly to King Island, famed for its fishing. It was in the middle of Bass Strait. He had agreed to pick up some crayfish to sell to friends. The trip was only a short hop.

The 20-year-old had limited experience in solo night flying, so he arranged to leave straight after college and filed his arrival time with King Island so that he would reach there before darkness closed in. He filled the tanks with many times more gas than needed, just to be sure.

But then, inexplicably, as his departure time drew close, the young aviator left the field for a leisurely meal. When he returned to the waiting aircraft night was closing in. He would now cross the ocean in the dark.

This puzzling decision has never been accounted for, because Valentich was about to take off on his final mission—a flight into oblivion.

All went well until the pilot passed a lighthouse by the coast. He was in steady contact with Steve Robey, on duty at Melbourne Air Traffic Control that evening. As Valentich soared out across the Strait he was alone in the empty sky with the speckled silvery sea just a few thousand feet below. He now had 30 more minutes of flying over water. If anything went wrong there would be no safe place to land.

At 7:06 P.M. Valentich called Robey to ask, "Is there any traffic in my area below 5,000 feet?"

Robey consulted his charts. There should be

nothing nearby, he told the pilot. But the small single-engined Cessna was far from alone. It was being tailed by a UFO.

Valentich spoke calmly of "Four bright . . . seems to me like landing lights . . . just passed over me—at least a thousand feet above."

The air traffic controller was baffled. What had "Delta Sierra Juliet"—call sign of the Cessna—just seen? *Nothing* else should be up there.

The pilot grew more concerned and reported, "It's approaching now from due east, towards me . . . . It seems to me that he's playing some sort of game . . . He's flying over me . . ." Then he cut in swiftly, "It's not an aircraft, it's . . . ." These mysterious words trailed away into the night.

Steve Robey checked every possibility, trying to keep the inexperienced aviator calm. He checked data on any military flights that might be over Bass Strait. There were none. What *was* up there?

The young pilot had by now regained some of his composure and told Robey what he was seeing. "It's a long shape . . . cannot identify . . . the thing is just orbiting on top of me . . . It's got a green light and sort of metallic-like . . . It's all shiny on the outside."

Then disaster struck. Valentich radioed that his engine was not working properly. He said he would try to make King Island. It was all he could do.

Suddenly, he cried out, "Ah, Melbourne—that strange aircraft is hovering on top of me again

. . . It's hovering and it's *not* an aircraft!" Then there was a frantic cry of the aircraft's call sign, a period when the microphone was open but no words were spoken, a weird metallic grinding noise—and then unbroken silence.

Cessna 182—"Delta Sierra Juliet"—had vanished from the skies.

A major search and rescue mission was launched when the aircraft failed to reach King Island. Despite several days of this, no trace of the plane or its pilot was ever found.

Ideas about what might have happened ranged from Valentich plotting his own disappearance and faking a close encounter to a fateful meeting with drug smugglers. There were, of course, also many rumors that Frederick Valentich had been snatched away by an alien spaceship.

The accident report, published in May 1982, merely concluded that nobody knew the truth. Very probably nobody ever will.

The Manhattan Transfer

Linda had been through this terrible nightmare before—the strange silence that invaded her bedroom, the eerie sense of knowing that something awful was about to happen, the tingling, tickling presence of that unknown force that had once taken over her life.

She had first seen the little grey-skinned creatures when she was a child. They had not seemed so terrifying then, but they were clearly not from Earth. Physically, they looked almost feeble and diminutive. In height they were a little more than four feet (1.2 m), although their heads were out of proportion to their bodies and teetered there as if they might fall off under their own weight. Then there were the eyes—huge, round and dark. When Linda looked into them, she felt cold—not an evil cold, but more one of scientists doing experiments with rats or mice, caring more about the outcome than about the methods they used.

They were experimenting on her, too. She knew that. But her memory was fuzzy, enhanced a little by regression hypnosis performed under the supervision of artist and UFO writer Budd Hopkins. He too lived in Manhattan, just across the city from her high-rise apartment. She had read one of his books, and then, in April 1989, she had gotten up the courage to talk with him.

From his work—hypnotic regression and meetings with other abductees—she now understood more about what was going on. There was an alien plan to develop hybrid babies formed of human genes intermixed with alien stock. It was Frankenstein in spacesuits. Yet, unlike the Gothic horror story, this was real life.

Now, seven months later, at about 3 A.M. on November 30, 1989, the visitors had come back. She was powerless to resist them. They could take her anywhere they chose and do what they would.

They were in her bedroom now. Horrified, she threw a pillow at one of them, but her body was numb and it fell short of its target. Then she collapsed onto the bed, completely paralyzed. In a blink of an eye, she was on the familiar table in the strange cold room with light flowing around her like liquid ice. They were coming at her with their probes and instruments. Then there was nothing.

Linda awoke in her bed, terrified that they might have harmed her family. She crept wearily out from under the bedclothes, energy drained from her being. Her husband and two children were immobile and dead to the world. Fear gripped her soul: Were they killed? Had the aliens murdered them? She got a mirror and held it up to their mouths. Gradually, slowly, breath came out and steamed up the glass. They were alive—deeply asleep, hopelessly unaware of what had happened.

The next morning, Linda called Budd and poured out her heart. He was kind to her, knowing how to coax her through the post-abduction trauma. Nobody in the world had more experience doing that. Eventually, she felt able to agree to more hypnosis. She needed to find out what they had done to her this time.

The images surrounded her mind. She saw herself, nightgown-clad, floating out through the closed window as if it had melted away. The creatures were all around her. They were holding her aloft with invisible beams, suspended in glowing light 12 stories above the streets of Manhattan, transferring her into their craft that hovered over the apartment rooftop.

That was it. One more case to add to the growing file that Budd Hopkins was collecting. Only this one was destined to be far more than that.

Fifteen months later, in February 1991, the abduction researcher received a startling letter. Letters arrived by the sackload week after week from all over the world—people suspecting that aliens might have spacenapped them, desperate to share their story with someone who would listen and not laugh.

But, this particular letter immediately struck a chord with Hopkins. It came from two men, Richard and Dan, who offered first names only and claimed to be New York police officers. They had lived with a terrible experience for some months now. One of them was so shocked he was on the edge of a nervous breakdown. He would sit in his car in a Manhattan street staring up at the top of an apartment block watching for *them* to return.

Then they told Budd what they had witnessed. In the early hours of November 30, 1989, they had seen a young woman in a nightgown float out of her 12th floor window in the presence of weird little creatures. They had taken her inside a saucer-like craft that sped away to the river, submerged completely and never came out again. They waited 45 minutes, praying that they would see her brought back. They did not.

Budd Hopkins was stunned. Never before had independent witnesses claimed to see a spacenapping *as it happened*. If this case could be verified it would undoubtedly be the most important one ever put on record. It could single-handedly prove that the aliens were really here.

However, the police officers refused to meet with Budd. They told him they could direct him to the room where the woman lived. They had been steeling themselves to go and check it out, but how do you approach a stranger and ask if she has ever flown out of her bedroom window into a spaceship? The UFOlogist, of course, did not tell them that he had no need to be directed to the spot. He already knew where Linda lived.

Richard and Dan supplied more details, including an audio tape, and then revealed the real reason for their reluctance. They were no ordinary policemen. In fact, they were bodyguards for a major political figure who was being transported to the New York heliport. But the car had stopped mysteriously on its own. The political figure had witnessed the entire thing. If he told the world about it, his credibility was such that everyone would listen.

Meanwhile, in 1991, a woman wrote to say that she had been driving over the Brooklyn Bridge at 3 A.M. on November 30, 1989, when all the lights and engines of the few cars that were crossing at that time simply failed, as did the streetlights on the bridge. Getting out to look at what was happening, she watched, along with several other drivers, as a woman floated out of her high-rise apartment into a UFO alongside several little creatures.

A third confirmation of the same incredible story was completely unprecedented. But again the evidence was almost impossible to verify. There was also the nagging question as to why the power failure was never recorded or why in over two years none of the occupants of the vehicles on the bridge had reported the matter to the police. And why were all of these stories finding their way to Budd Hopkins and none of them to anybody else?

If this abduction is honestly reported, as the witnesses allege, then it will be "the case of the century." But at present it relies exclusively on unsupported, often anonymous, testimony. A number of UFOlogists have attempted their own enquiries and learnt a few disquieting things. For example, a major newspaper office is opposite the site and people were working there at the time. Nobody saw anything. No one else in Linda's building was a witness, either. There were no records of helicopter flights that night. The trip that Richard and Dan's passenger had been taking is not recorded anywhere (they say it was a secret one). And, of course, the mysterious third man has not supported the story.

Rumors that Hopkins has not confirmed allege that the "third man" was Perez de Cuellar, former secretary general of the United Nations. De Cuellar's office has claimed that he was not in New York on the date in question. He himself has also denied any knowledge of the reported incident.

All that Budd Hopkins will say on this crucial matter is that he knows who the third man is. If and when that man reveals what happened, the world may change forever.

5. MARK OF THE UFO

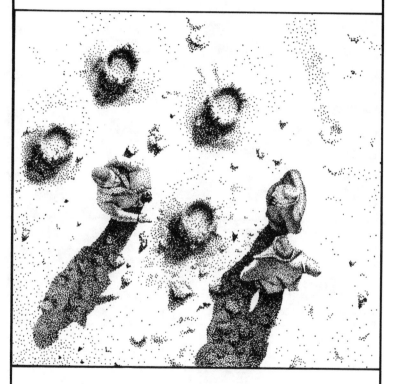

- Alien botanists?

- Cattle rustling—alien style . . .

- One of the best cases in UFO history—and one of the biggest coverups . . .

- A UFO is attacked by jet fighters . . .

The Boys in the Field

Farmer Maurice Masse had a bit of a problem. Somebody was stealing his lavender plants and he had no idea who it was.

Masse, a large, jovial man, had a piece of land at Valensole in the south of France, where he grew the sweet-smelling crop that was used to make scents and perfumes. But he kept finding patches of his fields bare, as if someone had been coming in at night and taking it all away.

One hot summer's morning in July, 1965, he was sitting beside his tractor planning the day's work when he noticed two boys standing in the field some distance away. It was not yet 6 A.M. and nobody up to any good would be in the middle of his field so early in the day, he suspected. He figured that at last he had caught the thieves and strode across the field to put a stop to their activities.

Maurice had assumed that the two strangers were children because of their small size—probably nine or ten years old. But the two were standing next to an odd-looking helicopter that had appeared from nowhere. This was puzzling.

Sometimes a military helicopter did land in Maurice's fields and he was not too happy about that, but as long as it stayed off his plants he didn't mind too much and would chat with the pilots. But this one was like none that had ever landed before. It was a white egg shape, about the size of a small car, and it sat on three little legs.

As he marched towards the boys and their peculiar device, Maurice quickly realized that these people were not children. In fact they did not even seem human. They were very strange-looking beings, with large bald heads, pasty faces and huge slanted eyes that stared out at him. They wore one-piece coveralls, and one had a tube-like instrument planted firmly by its side. It might well have been a gun!

As the farmer approached, the creature with the tube picked it up and pointed it straight at him. A light ray shot out of it and the farmer lost his balance as he stumbled backwards, toppling to the ground. Maurice knew right away that he had been hit. But this gun had fired no bullets. All it had done was freeze him into place, unable to move. He lay there rooted to the ground, helpless, as the strange creatures headed straight towards him.

After some time—he was not sure how long—Maurice began to regain his ability to move about, but he could not walk properly and felt weak and groggy. He heard a strange whistling noise echoing in his ears, which rose to a high pitch. Painfully glancing upwards, the stricken farmer watched the odd helicopter climb into the sky and fly away.

The lavender thieves had disappeared, taking some of his crop with them, presumably having left the way they came—inside their flying egg.

Maurice never forgot that day. He later admitted that he felt as if something else must have happened to him in the time that he lay on the ground. His memory of it was hazy and unclear, but it was there. He was not frightened by what had taken place, even though he suspected that he had been taken aboard the strange helicopter—that he had been "spacenapped."

For a long time he refused to talk about this part of his story even to his wife. All he would say was that the aliens would never make someone go aboard unless they had really wanted to do so. He, apparently, had been willing to help them in their explorations.

When shown a picture of what patrolman Lonnie Zamora saw at Socorro, New Mexico, just a year earlier, the farmer was thrilled. "Someone else has seen my UFO," he said excitedly. He was certain that it was the same object that had landed amid his lavender plants.

Maurice's farm, however, was never quite the same again. Although the thefts stopped, Maurice was never able to grow his crop again in the area where the UFO had landed. A large bare circle was left behind where the plants simply did not thrive. It was as if the earth had been affected by some kind of radiation.

Even years later, photographs taken at this landing spot revealed the same effect on the soil. The aliens had left their mark.

The Animal Mutilators

Near a town in Saga Prefecture in Japan, a farmer was awakened in the early hours of December 29, 1990, by the furious barking of his dog. The farmer ignored the animal, even though it never barked like that and it continued to bark for a long time. At 6 A.M. he was up and ready for the usual day's work, forgetting about the earlier noise. When he entered the cow shed, the farmer was amazed and upset to discover the mutilated corpse of a 12-month-old cow lying on the floor. Half its tongue was missing, and its four nipples had been cored out from its udder. There was no evidence of a struggle.

No further incidents occurred at that time. But when the dog started barking again, two years later on January 4, 1992, the farmer was not slow to investigate. Entering the cow shed, he saw a small white object, like a jellyfish, floating in the air. The object drifted outside where it vanished. A cow was discovered on the floor. It had a badly broken leg.

Bizarre animal mutilations are not new. A collector of odd stories, Charles Fort, recorded several from as long ago as 1810. The worst cases come from the U.S. They started with a horse called "Lady"—referred to as "Snippy" by a reporter who got the names mixed up.

Lady lived on a ranch near Alamosa in a remote area of Colorado's San Luis Valley. She was allowed to wander for miles through the clusters of chico bush. But every night she would turn up at the ranch house for a drink and a dole of grain. On September 8, 1967, she failed to appear. The following day, Lady's owner, Berle Lewis, and her brother, Ben King, went out looking for the horse.

What they found was horrific. The neck and head of the horse had been completely stripped of flesh. A later examination found that Lady's brain and other internal organs were missing. Some of the cuts were so clean they could only have been made with a scalpel.

Sheriff Ben Phillips suggested that lightning had killed the horse. Others thought the missing organs could have been eaten away by natural predators. Someone else had the idea that the horse was killed and mutilated by Satanists. But there were no tire marks nor any blood at the site. But strange "exhaust" marks were found and higher than normal radioactivity. News of the bizarre death of Lady—or Snippy—was to travel on the wire services around the world.

Berle Lewis was certain it was not a natural death. She and others had seen strange lights in the area. Her mother, Agnes, who lived nearby, told investigators that a large unknown object had passed over her cabin on the day Lady did not turn up for her feed. Berle told reporters, "I really believe that a flying saucer had something to do with Lady's death."

But this was only the start. During the 1970s over 10,000 head of cattle were discovered in the U.S. with organs surgically removed and *many* were drained of blood. The mutilations spread up into Canada and down into Puerto Rico, and some were reported in Spain. Since then there have been many other incidents in other countries. Were UFOs responsible for these inexplicable killings?

In May 1973, Judy Doraty, her daughter, Cindy, her mother and sister-in-law were driving back from Houston, Texas. The night was clearly illuminated by a full moon. Suddenly they saw a strange light hovering in the sky. At one point they climbed out of the car for a better look, then drove on.

Afterwards Judy began having headaches and

feelings of anxiety. UFOlogist Dr. Leo Sprinkle hypnotized Judy and asked her to remember the incident. It would seem that more happened than she could recollect in her normal waking state. In hypnosis, Judy told Dr. Sprinkle what she saw after she stopped the car:

"It's like a spotlight shining down on the back of my car. And it's like it has substance to it. I can see an animal being taken up in this. I can see it squirming and trying to get free. And it's like it's being sucked up."

Judy then felt she was in two places at the same time—still standing beside the car and also inside a strange craft. She watched in horror as some small beings took an animal—a calf—apart. Then Judy saw her daughter, Cindy, on the "operating table." She was afraid that "they" were going to do the same to Cindy!

"They don't listen, they just ignore me . . . go about their work as if it's nothing. They don't seem to have any emotions. They don't seem to care. They just take some samples from her. . . ."

Hypnosis does not act like a "truth drug." No one knows for sure whether Judy Doraty's experience in the craft really happened. Years later, when she was older, Cindy was also hypnotized. Her account was not as detailed as her mother's, but backed up parts of it.

In the meantime, weird animal mutilations are on the increase, most recently in Britain and Sweden, where hundreds of horses have been attacked.

The Night a Flying Saucer Crashed

Only two weeks after Kenneth Arnold saw what the press first called "flying saucers," a startled world learned that one of them had crashed. Almost as soon as this news hit the headlines, the U.S. military issued a strong retraction. They insisted that the thing that had crashed was not a UFO, but many people do not believe them.

The story began on July 2, 1947, when a rancher named William "Mac" Brazel was riding on horseback with his neighbor's son. They were in a remote area of Brazel's land some miles from the small town of Corona, New Mexico.

The night before, there had been a terrible storm and Brazel and his family had heard an earthshaking explosion. Brazel had gone out to search for damage, but what he found was stranger than anything he had imagined.

The two men trotted their horses into a large area of sandy ground covered in desert scrub. Something had clearly smashed down from above. There was a big groove dug into the earth as if an object had skidded along the surface. More peculiar still, huge pieces of debris were scattered over a large area. It looked as if a bizarre aircraft had fallen out of the sky.

As the two men investigated the wreckage, they quickly realized that this was no ordinary aircraft. The material on the ground was like nothing on earth. Some of the debris on Brazel's land was like canvas or parchment. Other pieces were as shiny as metal yet incredibly light. They felt like balsa wood to the touch, but were much more durable. Some bits even had odd symbols stained onto them in subdued purple and pink colors. They vaguely resembled Egyptian hieroglyphics or perhaps even Japanese writing.

Completely mystified, the horsemen collected some of the material and took it back to Brazel's homestead. They tried to put a dent into the metal with a sledgehammer. But even though it was easy to carry and could be flexed by hand, they could not make it bend out of shape for good no matter how hard they tried.

It took several hours to drive to Roswell, the nearest fair-sized town, but it had an air force base, which seemed the best place to report the matter. Roswell Air Force Base then flew top-secret nuclear bombers; it was the only base in the world to do so. The intelligence officer on duty was Major Jesse Marcel, and he was just as baffled by what he was shown as Brazel had been.

Marcel returned with Brazel to the crash site. Here they collected as much of the wreckage as they could, put it into a truck and took it back to the base. Brazel was asked to stay on in Roswell and help with the investigation. He was kept under guard for a week.

The base decided they had the proof to tell the world what had happened. After all, this was a historic event and nobody in Washington had given them any instructions on how to handle something as weird as this.

The teletypes clattered and the story hit the wires, informing the world that a "flying disk" had been recovered and was now at the air force base in Roswell.

But even as the wreckage was being flown on to what is now called Wright-Patterson Air Force Base in Dayton, Ohio, soon to be headquarters for all UFO investigations, official policy was changing back at Roswell. The base had received orders direct from Washington not only to stop releasing information but to send out a statement that there had been a big mistake—that there never was a flying saucer and that all the rancher had found was a beat-up old weather balloon. As a result, the story ebbed out of the news and was quietly forgotten by almost everybody except UFO enthusiasts.

Those who do not believe in the existence of UFOs have since tried to explain the wreckage as that of a Japanese balloon. During World War II, some of these were fitted with bombs and launched across the Pacific Ocean. A few did reach the U.S. The debris and strange writing upon the Roswell objects might support that theory. A balloon bomb might have lodged in a rocky crevice during the war and been exploded by a lightning strike two or three years afterwards.

On the other hand, according to testimony from some eyewitnesses, not only was the crash material genuine, but it was held for years in a top-secret complex at Dayton where scientists tried to rebuild the machine and figure out what made it fly.

There are many other stories about the Roswell UFO crash, including the claim that bodies of small alien creatures were found at another site nearby. These tales have never been verified, but a pilot claims he flew the bodies of four-foot-tall beings with egg-shaped heads from the crash site to a secret destination.

In January 1994, a senatorial investigation into the incident was opened with a search for any relevant documents that might have been suppressed by federal officials. Perhaps this will, at last, bring to light the truth about this remarkable case.

Nightmare over Teheran

Just after midnight on September 19, 1976, calls came in to the military control center at Teheran in the Middle Eastern state of Iran. A rather bored officer, B. G. Yousefit, listened impatiently to stories of a big white light beaming down onto the ground.

He told the excited witnesses on the phone that they were probably just watching a big star. It was nothing to worry about. They stopped calling, but Yousefit could not shrug off this growing problem. More calls came in, all repeating the same story. Maybe, he mused, just maybe, there is something up there—perhaps a helicopter with a searchlight. He reluctantly decided that he had better go outside and take a look.

Gazing out into the star-filled sky, the air force officer expected to see nothing. But he was wrong. He *did* see something—a huge, brilliant, glowing mass hanging above the outskirts of the city. Biting his lip, the Iranian called Shahrokhi Air Base and suggested that they launch a phantom jet interceptor as a matter of urgency.

At 1:30 A.M. the phantom took off under the control of Lieutenant Jafari, then 23 years old. Even from 70 miles away, he could see it dead ahead. The glare was exceptionally bright—like the sun going nova.

Jafari switched on the fighter's afterburners and pushed the jet through the sound barrier in pursuit of the UFO. The shock waves trailed across the tablelands that dropped towards the coast, shaking villagers from their beds to see the dazzling UFO for themselves.

Jafari was now closing in on the hovering object and radioed back his account: "It's half the size of the moon . . . radiating colors—violet, orange and white light."

But as he drew within a few miles of the monster, it shot away across the sky. He tried desperately to catch up with it, but the UFO easily outpaced him. Frustrated, he reported back to Shahrokhi base and they suggested that he abandon pursuit and return home.

Moments later, Jafari cried out: "Something is coming at me from behind. . . . It is 15 miles away . . . now 10 miles . . . now 5. . . . It is level now. I think it's going to crash into me. . . ."

There were long seconds of tension as ground control waited for the resolution. Was their pilot doomed? Relief came swiftly, a clearly stunned pilot announcing, "It has just passed by— missing me narrowly."

The terrified fighter pilot was shaken by this episode. Disorientated and confused, he had to be shepherded back to base. He explained that as he had tried to close in, his instruments lost all power for a few seconds. Only after he pulled out of the pursuit did his multimillion dollar equipment return to normal.

There seemed little doubt that this was intended as a sign to stay clear, perhaps the alien equivalent of a shot across the bow.

By now a second phantom had been launched and was on its way towards the UFO's location. The pilot locked on his radar intercept equipment. The jet was travelling at several hundred miles per hour. At this rate, it would catch up to the huge light in about 9 minutes.

However, as if it had detected that the radar lock was on, the UFO dramatically kicked into higher gear and shot away. The jet poured on its power, using afterburners to reach maximum velocity, but still it could not come close to matching the UFO's rate of departure.

Then the pilot and radar operator faced a moment of absolute terror. The UFO ejected a ball of light that swiveled around and headed straight for them. There was no way out. It looked as if the flying monster had fired a missile at the Iranian jet.

All air crew are trained to react instinctively in such a situation. The Iranian pilot instantly launched an AIM 9 missile at the UFO. Using its infrared heat-seeking capabilities it should have immediately honed in on the target and destroyed it.

But it did no such thing. The missile failed to launch. All power on the aircraft—radio communications, instrument readings, the lot—vanished the moment the pilot threw the switch to fire the missile. It was if someone knew what he was doing and was determined to put a stop to it, using far superior technology.

The ball of light ejected from the UFO was still bearing down on the defenseless aircraft. In another maneuver from the training manual, the pilot screwed the plane into a "negative G force" dive to evade the enemy missile. It was no use— the ball changed course, still heading straight for the phantom. It was now only four miles away. Impact was inevitable. The crew prepared for an emergency evacuation by firing their rocked-powered ejection switch—if it would only work!

Then a miracle happened. The glowing beachball-shaped mass swerved inside the twisting course of the diving jet, completed an incredible "U" turn and headed straight back to the UFO that had launched it.

There was absolutely no doubt to all concerned that they had just been giving a warning by forces that were far superior to themselves. Not for a moment did anyone think of launching a second missile, even when all power returned to the phantom moments later. Yet, as the jet plane pulled out of its dive, the UFO ejected a second ball of light, this time vertically downwards. As it streaked towards the ground like a firebomb, the air crew waited for the coming explosion to rock the night air.

Only there was no explosion. The ball simply oozed light as if it were a gigantic flare, illuminating a huge section of desert as if it were the middle of day. Seconds later, the UFO accelerated in an instant to an utterly fantastic speed and disappeared from view at thousands of miles per hour.

The dumbfounded crew of the phantom was ordered down to take a look at the object on the ground. They spiralled from 25,000 to 15,000 feet but could still see no substance behind the glow. Whenever they passed through a bearing of 150° on these circuits, the jet lost all communication power. Some weird interference signal appeared to be blocking it out. It was obviously coming from the thing on the ground. Unknown to the crew, at that moment a civilian airliner over Teheran had reported identical problems as it swept through 150° on its landing approach.

As the phantom reached 15,000 feet, the light simply went out, plunging the terrain into shocking darkness. The crew now faced another serious and unexpected problem. The brilliance of the glow that had saturated the night had been so bright for the past few minutes that their vision was severely impaired. The pilot was almost blinded with the afterimages burnt onto his retina as he stared into the dark sky. He could not fly the jet at all.

As a result, the fighter had to circle the sky for an hour under strict control from the ground until the pilot's vision returned sufficiently to allow them to make a safe landing at Shahrokhi.

At dawn the pilot and radar officer from the second phantom went out by helicopter to pinpoint the location where the huge glare had landed. It was a dried-up lake bed. They found nothing, but did detect a beeping noise on radio transmissions. In the area was a single isolated farmhouse, whose occupants reported hearing a big noise (probably the phantom jet) and seeing a blinding light through their bedroom window.

This case was taken very seriously. The U.S. Secretary of Defense compiled a secret dossier (later made public) calling its credibility "high" and saying it was "a classic which meets all the criteria necessary for a valid study of the UFO phenomenon." The UFO never came back.

Index